SUSTAINABLE WORLD
TRANSPORTATION

Rob Bowden

KIDHAVEN
PRESS™

THOMSON
★
™
GALE

San Diego • Detroit • New York • San Francisco • Cleveland • New Haven, Conn. • Waterville, Maine • London • Munich

For more information, contact
KidHaven Press
27500 Drake Rd.
Farmington Hills, MI 48331-3535
Or you can visit our Internet site at http://www.gale.com

Commissioning Editor: Victoria Brooker

Book Designer: Jane Hawkins

Consultant: Dr Rodney Tolley

Book Editor: Margot Richardson

Picture Research: Shelley Noronha, Glass Onion Pictures

Hodder Children's Books
A division of Hodder Headline Limited
338 Euston Road, London NW1 3BH

Title page: Separate traffic lanes in Amsterdam encourage the use of more sustainable forms of transporation.
Contents page: Traffic in Burkina Faso, Africa.

Picture credits: Cover: Jim Erickson/Corbis; Camera Press (Darren Jacklin) 8; James Davis Photography 37; EASI-Images (Rob Bowden) 12, 15, 31; Ecoscene (Nick Hawkes) 19, 30, (PJ) 33, (Adrian Morgan) 34; Eye Ubiquitous (Paul Scheult) 23; Impact (Caroline Penn) 3, (Piers Cavendish) 10, (Mark Henley) 15, (Stewart Weir) 18, (Mark Henley) 25, (Mark Henley) 32, (Philippe Achache) 42; Mouchel Consultants (Safer Routes to School Team) 40; Popperfoto (Reuters/Beawiharta) 7, (Reuters/Regis Duvignau) 12, Popperfoto (Reuters) 24, (Reuters/Greg Bos) 36, (Reuters/Marcelo Del Pozo) 38, Margot Richardson 28; Still Pictures (Mark Edwards) 1, (Mark Edwards) 4, (Shehzad Nooran) 5, (Mark Edwards) 9, (Mark Edwards) 11, (Mark Edwards) 16 (top), (Mark Edwards) 16–17 (bottom), (Mark Edwards) 17, (Mark Edwards) 20, (Jorgen Schytte) 21, (Ron Giling) 26, (John Maier) 27, (Mark Edwards) 29, (Dylan Garcia) 35, (Mark Edwards) 39, (Reinhard Janke) 41, (Thomas Raupach) 44, (Thomas Raupach) 45; Topham (Bob Daemmrich/The Image Works) 13, (Image Works) 22; Toyota Cars 14; Wayland (Jimmy Holmes) 6, 43.

LIBRARY OF CONGRESS CATALOGING-IN-PUBLICATION DATA

Bowden, Rob,
  Transportation / by Rob Bowden.
    p. cm. — (Sustainable world)
  Includes bibliographical references and index.
  ISBN 0-7377-1900-1 (lib. bdg. : alk. paper)
    1. Motor vehicles—Technological innovations. 2. Transportation. 3. Green
    Products. I. Title. II. Sustainable world (Kidhaven Press)

TL146.B684 2004
388.3—dc21

                                                        2003052949

Contents

Why sustainable transportation?

WE LIVE IN A WORLD WHERE MOBILITY is an essential part of our lives. Every day we make journeys: to school or to work; to stores; to movies or sports fields; and to visit friends and family. Some of these journeys are local, while others cover great distances. What is increasingly common to all of our journeys, however, is that we use some form of transportation to make them. Our decision to use transportation and our choice of transportation type are of great importance to the state of our environment, and to our health and well being.

The freeways in Los Angeles, California, are among the busiest roads in the world.

THINK FIRST

You may not think hard about your transportation choices, but there are good reasons to do so. For example, transportation is the fastest growing source of carbon-dioxide emissions that contribute to climate change. Congestion caused by transportation causes ill health and premature death for millions of people every year. And road traffic accidents kill up to one million people a year, most of them pedestrians. Transportation is also one of the fastest growing industries. The number of cars alone is expected to double between now and 2010 to over one billion! Such trends show that there are real reasons to be concerned about transportation and its impact on people and the environment.

These rickshaws in Bangladesh are a sustainable form of transportation because they use human energy for power.

ALTERNATIVE CHOICES

The future of transportation need not follow the trends of the last fifty years. There are alternatives. Many countries and individuals are now choosing to create more sustainable transportation: that is, transportation that does not cause harm to others or to the environment, both now and in the future. For example, walking is a completely sustainable method of transportation because it uses only human energy and produces no pollutants. Car use by contrast, is often completely un-sustainable as it uses non-renewable fossil fuels and is very polluting. The sustain-ability of other transportation alternatives such as cycling, trams and buses lies somewhere in between the extremes of walking and car use.

Central to the success of alternatives is choice: people must choose sustainable transportation for themselves. But to do this they must understand the problems of existing transportation and their options for the future. This book introduces some of those problems and presents options that will allow you to make better trans-portation choices for a sustainable world.

The transportation problem

Vehicles in less developed countries, such as Pakistan, are often adapted to carry as much as possible because motorized transportation is very scarce.

TRANSPORTATION is often considered vital for the progress and development of a country or region. Getting to basic services such as schools or hospitals can be difficult in areas where transportation facilities are lacking. In northern Kenya, for example, a lack of transportation means people may have to walk over 31 miles to reach their nearest health center and up to 9 miles per day to attend school. Where transportation has been improved, local communities have often benefited. For example, in Morocco, improvements to rural roads increased agricultural trade dramatically and more than doubled school attendance and hospital visits within just a few years.

A SECOND LOOK

Transportation provision is not always positive, however. The benefits of some forms of transportation are now increasingly outweighed by their costs, including pollution, congestion, and accidents. For example, in Asia it is estimated that 1.56 million people die each year due to atmospheric pollution, much of which comes from motorized transportation

These Indonesian children are wearing face masks to protect themselves from smog and smoke in busy traffic.

such as cars and buses. In the United States, meanwhile, up to two billion hours are wasted each year by people stuck in urban traffic jams and in the United Kingdom around forty thousand people are killed or seriously injured each year by accidents on the roads. Such costs have led many people to question the benefits of some transportation systems. For them, it is time to take a second look at our transportation options.

Many experts are concerned about the growing dependence on motor vehicles all over the world. Today, motor vehicles are the favored form of transportation for most people living in more developed, industrialized countries (North America, Europe, Japan, etc.). In Western Europe for example, the number of passenger cars more than doubled between 1970 and 1995, while road freight tripled. Motor transportation is also increasing rapidly in less developed regions as economies grow and incomes rise. Asia and Latin America have seen particularly fast growth, but in Africa car use is rising, but slowly.

CAR MANIA

Some cars, such as this convertible in Florida, are treated more as a fashion accessory than a form of transportation.

So why is motor transportation, and particularly the car, so popular? Well, for one thing, cars have become relatively cheap over the years as improvements in technology have reduced manufacturing costs and improved vehicle efficiency. But cars have also become something of a status symbol, often seen as a sign of wealth and success. In some societies they are almost fashion accessories with people changing their model or color as tastes change. Consider the latest trend in the United States for sport utility vehicles (SUVs), for example. In 1975, SUVs accounted for 20 percent of new car sales in the United States, but by 1999 this had risen to 46 percent. Such trends are encouraged by advertising and the motor industry spends more than any other on advertising — nearly $24 billion in 1998, over $14 billion of which was in the United States alone!

People believe that owning a car brings them freedom and opportunities; that they can go anywhere at any time. Car ownership has become a rite of passage in many countries with teenagers counting down the days until they get behind the

8

wheel and earn their freedom. This feeling is so strong that in one United Kingdom survey nearly three-quarters of young adults felt that the right to a driving license was more important than the right to vote. This obsession with the car has led some transportation experts to describe it as "car mania."

SKY HIGH

Since 1960, air travel around the world has increased by around 9 percent per year. By 2010 it is estimated that one billion people (15 percent of the world total) will be traveling by air each year. Air freight has increased even faster at around 11 percent per year. The problem is that air travel is very polluting. A passenger flying for eight hours contributes as much to global warming as an average person in India does in a year. With air travel set to grow dramatically the environmental costs could be sky high in the future.

> ### OPINION
>
> As I sit in traffic, windows rolled up against the fumes from idling exhausts, I wonder what happened to the freedom I once enjoyed.
>
> *Jim Motavalli, Sierra Magazine 1999*

The air around this airport in Mexico is thick with smog and pollution.

RAILWAYS IN DECLINE

Car and air travel have increasingly replaced rail as a form of transportation and so railways have, in many countries, declined in importance. In Kenya, Mexico, and South Africa, for example, rail travel declined by over 50 percent between 1980 and 2000. In other countries, including the United Kingdom, Japan, and France, the railway network has declined in size, too. In the United States, the rail network shrank by nearly 40 percent between 1980 and 2000 from 165,186 miles of track to 99,309 miles. The decline of railways is of particular concern because they are a more efficient and sustainable form of transportation than air or road travel. For example, over distances of less than 311 miles, rail travel produces three times less carbon dioxide than air travel.

UNEQUAL ACCESS

Of course, transportation problems are not limited to the type of transportation chosen. On a global scale there is the problem of unequal access to transportation. While most people living in more developed nations have many choices, people in less developed countries have little choice at all. For example, many women walk for over an hour and a half each day on essential journeys such as collecting water or fuelwood for their families. They may carry weights of over 44 pounds (often on their heads) and walk for several miles on each trip. For these women, and millions of others like them, the lack of transportation is a much bigger problem than the type of

Although rail travel is more sustainable than car travel, delays and crowding are common in big cities.

With limited access to affordable transportation, millions of people, such as these women in Africa, have only their own power to carry heavy loads.

transportation chosen. Even where transportation does exist it is not always affordable. For example, in Manila, the capital of the Philippines, the poorest residents may spend up to 14 percent of their income just to travel to work.

THE ROAD AHEAD?

People who currently lack transportation need reliable, safe, and cheap forms of transportation to improve their quality of life and well being. But, as many experts now agree, the model followed by the more developed nations — roads and car mania — is not a solution. Instead, people need to develop innovative and sustainable transportation solutions for the future.

Such thinking will also have to occur in the more developed nations if the hope of a more sustainable world is to be turned into a reality.

Developing sustainable transportation

ALTHOUGH THINKING ABOUT SUSTAINABLE transportation may be new for many people, some of the ideas and technology involved go back many years. For example, the light railways now being introduced into many urban centers are similar to tram systems that were first introduced in 1860 in London.

Similarly, electric cars, which are now on the verge of a comeback, originated in the late 1880s and in the United States were as popular as gas-powered vehicles until around 1920. Bicycles have an even longer history, dating back to 1791 and are still one of the most sustainable forms of transportation. Despite this long history, sustainable transportation systems have yet to be fully developed and are now relatively few and far between.

EFFICIENCY GAINS

To date, most of the effort toward creating sustainable transportation has been in the improve-

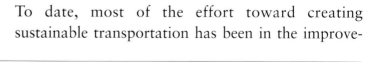

Top: An old trolley bus still runs in Birkenhead, United Kingdom, though it is now mainly a tourist attraction.

Left: A mechanic checks bikes in Bordeaux, France. These are loaned free of charge to the public to promote ecology-friendly transportation in the city.

12

Although sports utility vehicles (SUVs) are not fuel efficient, they continue to be a popular choice with many motorists.

ment of existing transportation options, particularly the efficiency of the car. This concern developed following a sudden increase in the cost of oil during the 1970s. By 1980 the price of crude oil (from which gasoline and diesel are derived) was ten times higher than in 1973. Several governments introduced measures encouraging manufacturers to make more fuel-efficient vehicles as a result. For example, the United States introduced the Corporate Average Fuel Economy (CAFE) program in 1975. The CAFE program sets average fuel-efficiency targets for new vehicles made by automobile manufacturers. If a manufacturer fails to meet these targets it is fined by the government. Partly as a result of such measures, an average U.S. family car today uses half the fuel of one built in 1975.

The CAFE levels are currently set at 27.5 miles per U.S. gallon (mpg) for passenger cars and 20.7 mpg for vans and light trucks (including SUVs), but some campaigners believe these are not high enough. They claim that if CAFE standards were raised to 45 mpg for cars and 34 mpg for light trucks carbon dioxide emissions would be cut by 600 million tons per year and the United States would save around 3 million barrels of oil per day! The technology to meet such standards already exists, but in recent years the fuel efficiency of U.S. manufacturers has actually been falling due to consumer preference for bigger gas guzzling vehicles.

The Toyota Prius contains both an electric motor and a gas engine. It aims to reduce emissions in urban driving and provide greater fuel efficiency.

TECHNOLOGY SOLUTIONS

Most improvements in the fuel efficiency of motor vehicles have come about through improved vehicle technology. Lightweight materials, such as aluminium and plastics, mean that vehicles are much lighter than in the past, but still as strong and safe. As weight is reduced the engine operates more efficiently. In fact, for every 10 percent reduction in weight, fuel efficiency increases by almost 6 percent. Other changes in car design have also improved fuel efficiency dramatically: better engines, improved tires, and better aerodynamics have all reduced the amount of fuel used. Despite this, experts suggest that the efficiency of many vehicles could be improved further by over 50 percent.

DATABANK

Only about 15 percent of the energy in fuel is actually used to move our vehicles. Most is lost as heat, or due to mechanical, road, and wind resistance.

CLEANER FUELS

The majority of motor vehicles are fueled by gasoline or diesel derived from oil. Oil is a non-renewable resource that is fast being used up in an energy-hungry world. Oil-based fuels are also very polluting. Their waste emissions contribute to climate change, acid rain, urban smog, and numerous health problems for humans.

One of the most serious health issues has been the use of lead in gasoline. Lead is toxic to humans and builds up in the body

Exhaust fumes contribute to the acid rain that has eroded details from this stone plaque in Stockholm, Sweden.

causing paralysis, blindness, brain damage, and even death. In more developed countries lead has been phased out of gas since the 1970s, but in many less developed regions it is still used. In some of Africa's major cities, for example, up to 90 percent of children suffer from lead poisoning. Another major pollutant, sulphur, has also been drastically reduced in modern fuels. Sulphur, when released into the atmosphere, contributes to acid rain, but the cleaner fuels now available have reduced emissions by up to 90 percent.

Cleaner fuels are not all good news, however. They still use oil and encourage car use. In more recent years some of the chemicals used in cleaner fuels have also become a cause for concern. In unleaded gas, for example, an additive called MTBE (methyl tertiary butyl ether) that helps engines run smoothly and reduces air pollution is thought to have links with cancer in humans and of having a damaging effect on wildlife. In the United Kingdom, MTBE has been blamed for a reduction in the number of house sparrows, one of the United Kingdom's most common birds.

Congested roads and poor quality vehicles, as here in Calcutta, India, can lead to high levels of air pollution.

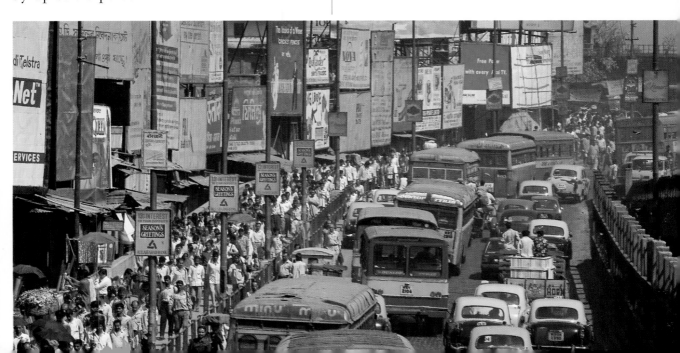

ALTERNATIVE FUELS

Concern about oil-based fuels has led to several alternatives being developed. Plant extracts have formed a particular focus of attention. In Brazil, for example, 40 percent of motor vehicles run on pure ethanol made from sugar cane, while the remainder run on a blend of ethanol (22 percent) and gasoline (78 percent). Bio-diesel is another plant-based fuel (made from vegetable oils) that is on the increase as both a pure and blended fuel. Bio-diesel is of particular interest because it can be used in existing diesel engines without them being modified. Plant-based fuels are renewable and release far fewer pollutants than oil-based fuels. However, they still release carbon dioxide — one of the most serious pollutants.

One alternative fuel now under development that releases no pollutants whatsoever is hydrogen fuel. By combining hydrogen with oxygen in a

Sugar cane is one crop used to make a less polluting and sustainable form of vehicle fuel.

special fuel cell it is possible to generate electricity for powering a vehicle and the only waste is clean, drinkable water. The problem is how to make the hydrogen. At the moment it is mainly produced from conventional fossil fuels and is therefore still polluting. It is possible to produce hydrogen from water, though, with oxygen as the only waste product. If the energy for hydrogen production came from renewable sources such as the wind or the sun then it would be possible to have near pollution-free motoring.

— **weblinks** —

For more information on alternative fuels, go to:
www.ncsl.org/programs/esnr/altfuel.html

Trams, cyclists, and pedestrians in Amsterdam, The Netherlands, show that transportation need not depend on cars.

BEYOND THE CAR

Improved vehicle efficiency and new fuels are undoubtedly making transportation more sustainable, but they are still focused on individual motor vehicles. The more sustainable projects are those that try to move beyond our reliance on the car. Light rail systems, for example, now provide a clean and efficient transportation option in an increasing number of cities. The most modern light rail systems can carry up to twenty thousand people per hour. To carry the same number of people by road would need a fifteen-lane highway! Cycle lanes have also been given greater priority in recent years. In Copenhagen, Denmark, a quarter of all city trips are made by bicycle.

DATABANK

Six bicycles typically fit into the road space used by one car. For parking, twenty bicycles occupy the space required for a single car.

A motorist in Brazil fills his car with alcool, a fuel based on ethanol that is extracted from sugarcane.

Park and Ride programs provide out-of-town parking lots. Drivers then travel into cities on public transportation, reducing congestion and pollution.

DESIGNED FOR LIFE

In European towns and cities up to a quarter of urban space is taken up by traffic. In Los Angeles, California — the car capital of the world — an incredible two-thirds of land is used for roads and parking lots. Such shocking figures have led many to call for a return to cities that are designed for life, not traffic. Throughout the world, town centers are being closed to traffic and returned to people. The impact this has on sustainable transportation is significant. In Strasbourg, France, for example, the banning of cars from the city center has led to bicycle use five times higher than in French cities where cars still have access. In Oxford, in the United Kingdom, daytime traffic dropped by 63 percent following restrictions to limit all but essential traffic from entering the city center. At the same time, improved buses and Park and Ride programs still allow people to reach the city for business or shopping. Such programs are likely to become more commonplace in the future.

PREPARED TO PAY

One approach to sustainable transportation has been to charge higher prices for those forms that are less sustainable. In Singapore, for example, an electronic road-pricing system automatically charges motorists using busy or congested roads. This encourages them to use public transportation instead and so reduces congestion and saves the driver money. As a result of this and other transportation policies, 63 percent of all motorized journeys in Singapore are made by public transportation. Road tolls are also common in France on some of its main roads and in the United Kingdom, motorists have had to pay to drive into central London since the introduction of toll fees in January 2003.

ROLE MODELS

Central to the development of sustainable transportation is the need for people to see how such a future might look and work. Without successful examples people may be reluctant to give up their current transportation choice. Two good role models are the cities of Freiburg in Germany and Curitiba in Brazil. Since the early 1970s both cities have developed transportation policies that are widely recognized as some of the most sustainable in the world. We'll consider these and other successful examples of sustainable transportation in the next chapter.

Road tolls such as these on France's freeways can help reduce traffic levels if they are correctly priced to discourage car use.

Sustainable transportation in practice

T HE INTEREST IN NEW FUELS and efficient technology is seen by many environmentalists as something of a false hope for sustainable transportation. They do not question that the doubling of fuel efficiency is of great benefit and that cleaner fuels are helping to clean our air. But what, they question, is the benefit of such measures if there are simply more and more motorized vehicles being used and more and more miles being traveled in them? The real future of sustainable transportation, so say most environmentalists, will depend on greater use of public transportation and zero-emission options such as bicycles and walking.

These separate traffic lanes in Amsterdam, The Netherlands, help to encourage more sustainable forms of transportation.

Privately owned *matatus* (minivans) wait to fill up before going to various city center destinations in Kampala, Uganda.

GOING PUBLIC?

Public transportation plays an important role in most countries, though this varies dramatically across the world. For example, in Japan around 46 percent of motorized journeys are currently made by some form of public transportation, whereas in the United States it is just 2 percent! In less developed countries where incomes are generally much lower, public transportation is often the main or only form of motorized transportation available to people. In East Africa, for example, local minibuses or pick-up trucks, known as *matatus*, are the main form of motorized transportation with bigger buses operating only on intercity routes.

Throughout the world, however, there has been a trend toward less use of public transportation. This is because incomes have risen and personal car use has grown. In South Korea, for example, a tripling of incomes between 1980 and 1995 saw the number of privately owned motor vehicles increase by an amazing 2,216 percent. As fewer people use public transportation, routes and frequency are reduced and vehicles fall into disrepair. This in turn makes public transportation less attractive and may persuade those using it to use their own vehicles. In rural areas of the United Kingdom and on the outskirts of many towns such trends led to a virtual collapse of bus services that until the mid-1950s were the main form of passenger transportation. (Today, buses account for just 6 percent of U.K. passenger trips.) In recent years, however, congestion and environmental concern have been slowly changing attitudes toward public transportation.

DATABANK

There were 532 million cars in use globally in 2000. This is twice as many as in 1975 and ten times the number in 1950.

A previously discontinued train service returns to New York.

GROWING DEMAND

Many countries are currently experiencing a growth in demand for public transportation for the first time in several decades. In Denmark, for example, bus travel increased by over 40 percent between 1980 and 1998, while the number of rail passengers in the United Kingdom grew by almost 30 percent over the period 1986 to 2001. In the United States too, public transportation has registered growth for the first time in many years and outstripped the growth in car use in both 1999 and 2000. So why is public transportation suddenly becoming more popular?

Congestion and pollution are two reasons why many people are returning to public transportation. In some of the most congested cities public transportation is now the fastest way to get around. For example, in the city of Manila in the Philippines it takes about 15 minutes to travel 14 miles using the tramway, a journey that by motor car would take up to 2 hours! Such differences are achieved by giving public transportation such as buses and trams their own lanes and priority over cars at junctions or traffic lights.

FRIENDLY DESIGNS

Modern buses and trams have been redesigned to make them more people-friendly. They have wider doors for easier and faster boarding, lower floors to ease access for the elderly, disabled, or those with young children, and more comfortable seating than in the past. Many systems now include passenger information both at stops and on board the vehicles themselves. This helps people to better plan their journeys and means they know how long they will have to wait before the next service arrives. It has been estimated that around 20 percent of public transportation journey time is taken up by waiting at stops, so any reduction in this will make public transportation far more attractive to use.

DATABANK

An average car in Bangkok, Thailand, is estimated to spend up to forty-four days a year stuck in traffic and yet new cars are being added at up to four hundred per day!

Video screens at this bus stop in Bangkok, Thailand, provide waiting passengers with information and entertainment.

Better integration of different transportation systems has also helped make public transportation more user-friendly. In cities such as Vienna, Austria, London, United Kingdom, and Stockholm, Sweden, a single ticket allows passengers to transfer between transportation modes (such as trains, buses, and light railway) for each stage of their journey.

LIGHT RAILWAYS

Among the fastest growing forms of sustainable transportation are light rail systems. These are rail systems that run above ground using tracks sunk into existing roads or, alternatively, on specially elevated tracks. These elevated systems are sometimes referred to as sky-trains and operate in Vancouver, Canada, London, and Kuala Lumpur, Malaysia, to name a few. Many of the most advanced light rail systems now operate automatically. Two of the oldest such systems operate in Kobe, Japan and in Lille, France. The Lille system began service in 1983 and today carries over 230,000 passengers per day. The computer automation means it is punctual and reliable with services departing every five minutes and once a minute during peak times. Safety has also been improved using driverless trains as most accidents on such transportation systems tend to be due to driver error.

One advantage of light rail is that, because it runs above ground, it costs less to build than an underground (subway) system. This means light rail has been especially popular for smaller or less wealthy cities. In Germany, for example, more than fifty cities have light rail systems. In less developed countries, cities such as Bangkok, Kuala Lumpur, and Manila, The Philippines, all have successful and expanding systems. More cities are now turning to light rail as a part of their solution to transportation congestion. In the United Kingdom, Nottingham is one of the latest cities to do this. In 2003, the Nottingham Express Transit (NET) will eliminate an estimated two million car journeys from the city's roads every year.

In cities of over 1 million people, however, full-size underground systems may be more suitable for mass transit than a light rail system. The New York subway has been running since 1904 and today operates 6,500 services a day, carrying 3.1 million passengers on 25 interconnected lines. The subways in Moscow and Tokyo, though newer, each carry over 7.5 million passengers per day! Both subway and light rail systems require heavy investment and a reliable electrical supply. This means they are not always suitable for less developed countries.

Tokyo's highly efficient subway system carries over 2,700 million passengers per year.

BACK TO THE BUSES

Buses are the most widely used form of public transportation with around one billion journeys being made globally every day. Buses are more flexible than rail systems because they do not require great investment in infrastructure (rails, signals, platforms, etc.) and can run on even the bumpiest of dirt roads. In many less developed countries buses are the main form of intercity transportation departing numerous times a day and stopping to pick up and drop off people on demand. Smaller buses (or minibuses) then transfer people from the main bus route and take them to smaller settlements or isolated locations. Such systems work well and provide people with an affordable means of travel.

Buses can also provide effective city transportation, though this normally depends on how free their route is kept. In many cities, buses now have their own lanes and priority at intersections and signals. Making bus travel faster can attract people away from their cars. One of the best examples of bus priority comes from Curitiba, Brazil. There, central bus expressways provide quick and reliable transportation to all areas of the city along five central corridors. Cars are kept to the edge of the corridors so that there is no congestion or delays for the buses. This simple priority system, combined with modern bus design and flat rate charges, means that almost 70 percent of Curitiba's population use the buses each day.

In rural areas scheduled bus services are not always an efficient form of transportation. Buses can run their entire route with very few passengers and may not go to where passengers need them. In the remote highlands of Scotland new flexible bus routes have been introduced so that passengers can request to be picked up or dropped off at locations close to, but not always on the main route. Dial-a-Bus programs have also been introduced for people to arrange pick up by the nearest available vehicle at a time that suits them best. Such systems make better use of available transportation resources, a key priority for a more sustainable future.

In Curitiba, Brazil, buses have their own priority transportation route while cars are kept to separate outside lanes.

DATABANK

Curitiba, Brazil's highly organized bus transit system can carry an incredible two million passengers per day!

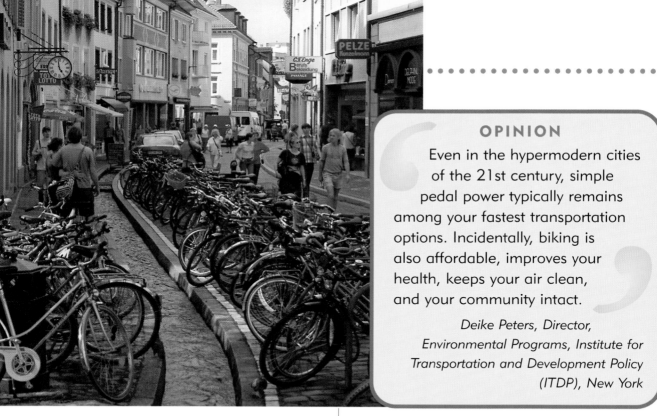

Following local government intervention, many commuters and city residents in Freiburg, Germany, now prefer to travel by bicycle.

PEDAL POWER

Besides walking, cycling is the main form of non-motorized transportation used in the world. China alone has over 400 million bicycles and in some cities nearly 80 percent of journeys are completed by bicycle. In East Africa, bicycle taxis, known as *boda bodas*, are a popular form of transportation in non-hilly regions. And it is not just in less developed countries that bicycles are popular. In Denmark, around 20 percent of all trips are made by bicycle and this rises to 30 percent in The Netherlands where there are over 11,800 miles of bicycle lanes.

Priority bicycle lanes, the banning of cars from city centers, and bicycle parking facilities have all contributed to a recent increase in cycling in many European cities. In Freiburg, Germany, for example, bicycle lanes were increased from just 18 miles in 1970 to over 310 miles by 2001 and over 5,000 secure bicycle parking spaces have been provided. This has led to bicycles being used for over a quarter of Freiburg's journeys. The United Kingdom and United States have much lower bicycle use but are now trying to make cycling a more attractive option. In the United States, an East Coast bicycle trail stretching 2,610 miles is nearing completion and in the United Kingdom the national bicycle network had reached over 6,600 miles by mid 2002 with a further 3,400 miles of routes planned by 2005.

Cycling is not always the most practical form of transportation as there are limits to what can be carried and in poor weather the rider is exposed to the elements. Innovative ideas are helping to overcome such limitations, however. In the London borough of Tower Hamlets, for example, specially adapted rickshaw taxis (based on the Indian models) have been introduced to try to reduce motorized transportation by a third. They can carry two adults and a child and come complete with rain hoods and even blankets to cope with the British weather! A specially extended bicycle called an ExtraCycle allows traders in South Africa and Kenya to carry produce to and from market, making it much easier than on a normal bike. The U.S. company that invented the ExtraCycle also sells it in the United States as a Sports Utility Bike, able to carry surfboards, camping equipment, friends, or even pets!

---

weblinks

For more information on the national cycling network in the United States, go to www.bikeroute.com

---

Pedal rickshaws provide an interesting adaptation of the bicycle and are a relatively quick way of traveling around New York's busy streets.

DATABANK

In the year 2000, world bicycle production climbed to 101 million, more than double the 41 million cars produced.

INTEGRATED TRANSPORTATION

Many transportation systems are planned individually with little thought for the needs of passengers to transfer between different travel modes. In many towns and cities, for example, the central bus station may be some distance from the rail or subway systems. Similarly, facilities for cyclists to safely leave their bicycles are often poor at rail, bus, or subway stations. Such conditions can deter people from using public transportation and encourage car use as it seems more convenient and faster.

Many transportation experts believe that until such problems are resolved it will be difficult to persuade people to leave their cars. They argue that there is a need for integrated transportation systems that give public transportation networks the same freedom and ease of use that people associate with private motor cars. Many countries are now adopting such approaches and some have already proved very successful. In Stockholm, Sweden, for example, the subway, rail and bus networks operate from a central building allowing easy transfer for passengers between the different transportation modes. Clear signs and transferable tickets allow the system to operate with little waiting time for passengers. Even the ferries that travel

Travelers arriving at the central station in Stockholm, Sweden, can conveniently choose a train, bus, or taxi to continue their journey.

Integrated transportation in Sweden: A local bus waits for a ferry so that passengers will not have to wait before continuing their journey.

between Stockholm's numerous islands are integrated with local bus services that wait to meet the ferry and collect passengers at the main stopping points.

One way to improve use of public transportation is to improve timetables for different services so that they are better integrated. Waiting times can make a journey by public transportation up to twice as long as by private vehicle. In the Austrian city of Graz, routes, timetables, and fares for all forms of public transportation are coordinated by a single organization. This helps to reduce waiting times and improve journey times significantly. As in Stockholm, a single station provides connections between different transportation modes including facilities for cyclists to safely store their bicycles.

In Germany, the rail network has actively promoted bike and rail services by increasing the space available for cycles to be carried on trains in specially designed compartments. Brochures and a bicycle hotline provide cyclists with information about appropriate services. This helped to double the number of bikes carried on German railways, to over 1.6 million per year within a decade. Caltrain in California introduced a free Bikes-on-Board program in 1992 and now offers a bike carriage on every commuter train, carrying a total of some two thousand bicycles per day in 2002.

Making sustainable transportation work

CREATING THE TECHNOLOGY and infrastructure to make transportation more sustainable is only a small part of the problem. Much harder is the task of convincing people to use such systems as part of their daily travel plans. The dominance of the car has become part of society itself. In countries where car use is currently low, such as China, cars are seen as a symbol of success and their use is growing rapidly. In fact, in many Chinese cities (especially Beijing and Shanghai), preference is being given to improving road networks while existing sustainable transportation options such as cycling are being restricted. So what can be done to make sustainable transportation work?

PAYING THE PRICE

One of the simplest suggestions to make transportation more sustainable is simply to charge according to its real cost. The real cost includes not just the running costs, but also the cost of damage to the environment or people's health. Using such methods, cars and other gasoline- or diesel-driven vehicles would become

China is building new roads to encourage car use and discouraging cyclists from entering some city centers.

Two-seater Smart cars have ultra-low carbon dioxide emissions and so qualify for lower road taxes in the United Kingdom.

relatively expensive to use and people may be encouraged to use alternatives such as public transportation or walking and cycling. Introducing such charges is not easy, however. Many governments have adopted alternative ways of charging for less sustainable transportation types. In the United Kingdom, for example, new cars are taxed according to the amount of carbon dioxide they emit. The cleaner the car the less the annual road tax costs. Taxes on fuel are also used to promote sustainability. In 1989, for example, fuel that contained lead was taxed in the United Kingdom to make it more expensive and to persuade people to switch to cheaper and cleaner unleaded gas. Before the introduction of the tax on leaded fuel, only 1 percent of vehicles in the United Kingdom used unleaded fuel, but within a year of its introduction this had risen to 25 percent. Fuel taxes are also said to persuade people not to use their cars, but in the United Kingdom where 76 percent of the fuel price is government tax, car use remains high and traffic is predicted to double by 2025. Elsewhere, governments have introduced more targeted forms of charging to encourage more sustainable transportation use and others are now following their example.

> ## OPINION
>
> Taxes on motorists should be tripled to reflect the true cost of road transportation, which adds 11 billion pounds a year to health bills because of exhaust pollution.
>
> *The British Lung Foundation 1998*

TARGETED CHARGES

Targeted charges make less sustainable forms of transportation more expensive and encourage changes in transportation use. In the United Kingdom, for example, a driver using a car on quiet rural roads is charged the same road tax as one using it in busy city traffic. Studies show, however, that the cost to society (pollution, health effects, noise, etc.) is twenty-five times higher for the urban driver. By targeting urban drivers, where alternative transportation options are normally at their best, it is hoped that urban car traffic can be significantly reduced. From January 2003 cars in London had to pay $8 a day to enter central areas of the city. A survey in May 2002 suggested that half of London's car drivers would change their travel habits following the introduction of the charge. Similar programs operating in Singapore and Salzburg, Austria, have been successful in encouraging motorists to switch to public transportation or walking and cycling instead. Such programs are only practical, however, if alternative forms of transportation are available. It is the lack of alternatives that makes people critical of such charges.

Drivers must pay a toll to travel in Singapore's restricted zone near the center of the city.

TRANSPORTATION EFFICIENCY

Greater transportation efficiency is being promoted by several governments. In New Zealand, Iceland, Norway, and Sweden, for example, lorries (moving trucks) are charged according to the weight they carry and the distance travelled. This promotes the more efficient use of lorries, many of which would otherwise travel around half empty. In the United Kingdom, 81 percent of annual freight traffic is carried by road, but around 30 percent of the lorries on U.K. roads are empty at any one time!

Another efficiency option includes special lanes for high occupancy vehicles (HOVs). These allow vehicles carrying more than one passenger (often a minimum of three) to use a separate lane to other traffic in order to speed up their journey time. In Los Angeles, one of the first cities to introduce HOV lanes in 1973, 35 percent of the freeways are now set aside for HOVs. Similar programs operate in forty other North American cities and several Australian ones. The United Kingdom has been experimenting with HOV lanes since 1998. If successful it could be significant as U.K. studies have shown that 70 to 80 percent of car commuters travel on their own — an extremely inefficient form of transportation.

Many cargo trucks are empty for some of their journeys and so are an inefficient form of transportation.

A theater group in Seville, Spain, promotes alternative forms of transportation during Europe's annual Car-Free Day.

PROMOTING ALTERNATIVES

Discouraging people from using cars does not always work and can be abused by some motorists. In Los Angeles, for example, people have been caught using inflatable passengers in order to use carpool lanes and fool the authorities. Transportation campaigners suggest that there is a need for more direct promotion of alternatives and restraint on motorized traffic if gridlock is to be avoided. Some new ideas are now in practice around the world. These include bans on cars entering city centers, government funding for public transportation, and education campaigns to make people aware of their transportation choices and the effect they have.

In Europe, for example, the annual car-free day started in La Rochelle, France, in 1997. It quickly spread to include over one thousand towns and cities across the continent by 2001. Each year on September 22, governments and town authorities close down streets to motorized traffic, and pedestrians and cyclists take over the streets. Events are held to promote awareness of sustainable transportation and from 2002 onward several European cities will extend these activities

Every day thousands of shoppers enjoy walking along car-free Grafton Street in Dublin, Ireland.

as part of the new European Mobility Week (September 16–22). This will raise awareness of public transportation services and show the importance of returning cities to the people who live in them and not the car.

As we have already learned, several cities have near permanent car-free policies for part or all of the day (see pages 18–19). Where these have been introduced businesses have benefited as more people enjoy the pleasures of shopping and doing business in a cleaner, quieter and safer environment. Zurich, Switzerland, is living proof that adopting sustainable transportation need not harm the economy as many fear. Yet governments and city authorities often seem reluctant to crack down on car use, believing it will make them unpopular with voters. This can be seen in government spending on transportation at a national level. In the United States for example it is estimated that $108 billion was spent on streets and highways in 1998 compared with just $26 billion on public transportation projects.

weblinks

For more information on the European Mobility Week campaign, go to www.mobilityweek-europe.org

OPINION

More and more of Europe's streets are ugly corridors dominated by traffic, noise, parked cars and highway engineering. Let us re-establish them as places where people young or old play, meet, chat, kiss, snooze, drink, eat or walk the dog. We need to turn the tide of motor traffic and create 'living streets.'

European Mobility Week Website, 2002

Protesters block a busy street in London during a demonstration to "reclaim the streets."

PUBLIC OPINION

Despite government fears, recent surveys suggest that many people would be happy to see less car use. In Strasbourg, France, for example, two-thirds of motorists believe that cars in towns will soon become a thing of the past and that the city should rightly belong to pedestrians, cyclists, and public transportation only. In the United Kingdom a recent survey showed that around 40 percent of people believed transportation was the biggest problem in their local area and that the government was not doing enough about it. Over half supported greater use of programs such as priority bus lanes and a quarter of motorists said they would use the bus if journey times could be reduced.

CHANGING BEHAVIOR

Such results are encouraging for sustainable transportation, but turning them into a reality is much more difficult. One of the greatest challenges is to change people's attitudes and behavior to public transportation, especially in cultures where the car has become such a status symbol. In some countries, ride sharing and carpools have been introduced to remove the emphasis on everyone having their own vehicle. The car pool owns a number of vehicles. Members can arrange to borrow a car for a short period when they need one. This encourages people to better plan their use of the car for essential journeys only and to walk for journeys over shorter distances. By having different types of vehicles available in the pool, members can also select the most appropriate vehicle for each use.

Italy is the latest country to join the European Car Sharing Association with fleets of electric vehicles in several cities including Rome and Milan. Customers are given a magnetic card and can collect one of the electric cars from special parking areas all over the city. They pay for the service according to the distance driven. More than 550 towns are involved in the European Car Sharing Association and by 2003 it is predicted to have over 350,000 car-sharers. Such programs show how relatively small changes in personal behavior (simply giving up personal car ownership) can make great contributions toward sustainable transportation.

DATABANK

Studies have shown that an average car may be parked for as much as 95 percent of its lifetime.

Providing parking for commuters and city residents uses up enormous areas of valuable urban land.

Sustainable transportation and you

EACH OF US MUST TAKE PERSONAL responsibility for our own transportation choices if a sustainable transportation future is to become a reality. It is of little use complaining about pollution, congestion, poor health, and environmental damage if each time we go to school, work, or the store we hop into the family car.

A Walking Bus program in England gets younger children safely to school.

TAKING IT PERSONALLY

A study in Grenoble, France, found that 50 percent of children living within 1,300 feet of their school and 80 percent of children living within 2,600 feet travelled there each day by car!

OPINION

Parents are rightly worried about the safety of their kids on our crowded roads. But putting even more children into cars is not the answer. It's bad for the environment, bad for their health, and can threaten the safety of others. Walking Bus schemes [programs] could be the answer.

Tanya Jowett, Friends of the Earth, Maidenhead, United Kingdom

To reduce these figures, walking-bus and cycling-bus programs were introduced. These provide safe routes for children to get to school whereby volunteers (normally parents) take turns accompanying a group of children to and from school by either walking or cycling. One volunteer is the driver (at the front) and the other the conductor (at the back) and the route can be varied to pick up and drop off children along the way. Similar schemes also operate in the United Kingdom, New Zealand, United States, and Canada and have been shown to not only reduce traffic, but to increase the health of the children involved.

You can take responsibility for your own transportation choices by choosing the most sustainable method possible. This will often be walking or cycling. In the United Kingdom, for example, a quarter of all car trips are less than 1.5 miles — easy walking distance for most people. Where longer journeys are necessary, find out about public transportation options, or at the very least try to share your journey with others if you have to go by car.

One type of travel you have little choice over is if you fly somewhere. However, even this can be made more responsible by paying a small fee to offset the carbon dioxide emitted during your flight. A company called Climate Care will invest your payment into projects that neutralize carbon-dioxide emissions such as tree planting or distributing low-energy light bulbs. At just $1.58 per hour of air travel for each person this program adds only $47 to the cost of an average family vacation — not much for a more sustainable future.

Passengers checking in at Hamburg airport in Germany could pay a voluntary tax to reduce the environmental impact of their flight.

— weblinks ⟩ —

To find out more about Climate Care, go to www.co2.org

These passengers on the Eurostar train service between the United Kingdom and mainland Europe have time and space to enjoy a meal, read a book, or just enjoy the scenery.

When you become an adult you will have even more power to make your transportation choices sustainable. For example, by choosing where to live and work you can minimize the need for travel, and you can make sure that if you need to travel you have access to public transportation services. If you live in an area with good transportation links you may want to think twice before getting a driving license. Do you really need it? Think of all the money you could save in tax, fuel, and car maintenance costs! If you travel long distances with your family then think about using the train. By planning ahead you can normally get guaranteed seats and cheaper fares. You could even plan your family vacation by rail, bus, or boat as a more sustainable way to travel than by air. It can also be more relaxing with time to enjoy the scenery or read a good book.

DON'T LOOK BACK!

Most importantly you should act now so that you do not look back in several years and wonder how the world around you has become even more congested and polluted than it used to be. The examples in this book show that there are transportation alternatives that not only bring us personal freedom, but also a cleaner, healthier, and more people-friendly environment in which to live. This is surely what we want not only for ourselves, but for future generations — your children and grandchildren.

For short distances and local travel, bicycles are a healthy, fun, quick, and easy choice.

LOCAL ACTION
Doing your part

There are many different ways in which you can contribute to sustainable transportation. Here are a few ideas to get you started.

- Think before you travel and use the most sustainable method available.

- Find out about public transportation in your area.

- Walk or bicycle to school, or join a walking- or cycling-bus program.

- Share lifts with friends and other family members if you use the car.

- Join a group campaigning for more sustainable transportation.

- If you have a family car, make sure it is as efficient as possible.

- Work with your school to improve transportation options to and from school.

- Share your knowledge about sustainable transportation with friends and family.

The future of sustainable transportation

EXAMPLES FROM AROUND THE WORLD show us what a future focused on sustainable transportation might look like and many of these have been featured in this book. We have also seen the importance of government and individual commitments to improving transportation choices and learned how we can each do our own part. Despite these positive examples, we are faced with a world that is becoming ever more congested and polluted by the dominance of motorized transportation and its reliance on fossil fuels.

HOPEFUL SIGNS

There are signs that governments, businesses and individuals around the world are finally getting serious about transportation issues. Major car companies are investing in cleaner technology such as hydrogen fuel cell vehicles (see pages 16–17), and many businesses are doing their part to improve their own transportation needs such as using electric vehicles or providing better facilities for

A driver recharges the batteries of his electric car in Germany using sustainable energy provided by solar panels.

As more people use public transportation like these German trams, support for such services will improve in the future.

cyclists. The best signals come from those cities where the private automobile is being rejected in favor of public transportation and greater access for people. These cities, such as Zurich, Switzerland, Freiburg, Germany, and Copenhagen, Denmark, are the best indication yet that sustainable transportation can bring about a better future for all.

IN YOUR HANDS

In truth, though, the future of sustainable transportation is in the hands of individuals like you and me. New technology and government policies can provide us with the tools and incentives for sustainable transportation, but whether or not these are turned into a reality will depend on our personal choices. As citizens, we have the power to influence businesses and governments through the decisions we make, the programs we support, and the problems that we stand up to. The more that public transportation is used, for example, the more likely companies are to invest in new routes or more frequent services. In turn this is likely to increase the appeal of public transportation to others.

You also have the power to influence others by educating them about sustainable transportation and encouraging them to make better transportation choices. Each of us must take this responsibility seriously if we are to develop transportation systems for life in more sustainable world.

Glossary

Acid rain Produced when pollutants such as sulphur dioxide and nitrogen oxides (emitted when fuels are burned) mix with water vapor in the air.

Aerodynamic A shape that is designed to reduce the effects of air resistance.

Climate change The process of long-term changes to the world's climate (warming or cooling, etc). Occurs naturally, but today is more as a result of human activities polluting the atmosphere.

Congestion Where vehicles overcrowd a street or road making movement difficult or impossible for some time.

Developed countries The wealthier countries and continents of the world including Europe, United States, Canada, Japan, Australia, and New Zealand.

Emissions Polluting waste products (gas and solids) released into the atmosphere. These include carbon, sulphur, and lead from car exhaust fumes.

Ethanol A colorless liquid, produced from fermented carbohydrates such as sugar cane.

Fossil fuels Fuels from the fossilized remains of plants and animals formed over millions of years. They include coal, oil, and natural gas.

Fuel efficiency Whereby improvements in vehicle design and fuel mean that vehicles can travel further on the same amount of fuel.

Global warming The gradual warming of the earth's atmosphere as a result of greenhouse gases, such as carbon dioxide and methane, trapping heat.

Gridlock When congestion affects a wider area than usual so that vehicles are unable to move in any direction at all.

Infrastructure Networks that enable communication and/or people, transportation, and the economy to function such as roads, railways, electricit, phone lines, and pipelines.

Integrated transportation systems The coordination of different forms of transportation (buses, trains, trams, cars, etc.) to improve people's mobility and reduce pollution in the environment.

Light railway Small-scale railways that run on sunken or elevated tracks.

Mass transit The transition (movement) of large numbers of people.

Mobility The ability to move from one location to another, e.g. for leisure or work.

Motorized transportation Any form of transportation which has a motor fitted to it, but usually means road vehicles.

Non-renewable resource Resources that once used are gone and cannot be replaced except over millions of years. These include coal, oil, and natural gas.

Public transportation Passenger vehicles, e.g. buses, trains and trams, running on set routes, at set times and fares.

Renewable resources Resources that are easily replaced or replace themselves to be used again. The sun is a renewable energy resource because it can be reused every day.

For further exploration

Rite of passage An event that marks a significant time in someone's life.

Smog A mixture of fog, smoke, and air-borne pollutants such as exhaust fumes.

Sports utility vehicle (SUV) A vehicle (normally four-wheel-drive), designed specially for use on rough ground, but used mostly for everyday driving.

Sustainable transportation Transportation systems that meet the needs of today's global population without causing harm to people or the environment, both now and in the future.

Zero emission Vehicles, such as bicycles, that do not release any polluting waste products.

Books

Andrew Church and Amanda Church, *Earth Alert!: Transport*. London: Hodder Wayland, 2001.

Paul Dowswell, *Great Inventions: Transport*. Barrington, IL: Heinemann Library, 2002.

Andrew Nahum, *Children's Encyclopedia of Transport: On the Move*. London: Marshall Editions, 2001.

Websites

www.earthday.net

The Earth Day Network provides information on various types of environmental programs, including information on worldwide car-free days and events.

www.greenfleet.com

The Greenfleet website offers information on sustainable transportation, the impact of transportation on the environment, and a discussion of the Kyoto conference regarding energy. A bit high-level, but clearly organized.

Index